HIP-HOP ARTISTS

POST MALONE

RAPPER, SINGER, AND SONGWRITER

BY MARCIA AMIDON LUSTED

Essential Library

An Imprint of Abdo Publishing
abdobooks.com

ABDOBOOKS.COM

Published by Abdo Publishing, a division of ABDO, PO Box 398166, Minneapolis, Minnesota 55439.

Printed in the United States of America, North Mankato, Minnesota.
102019
012020

THIS BOOK CONTAINS RECYCLED MATERIALS

Cover Photo: KGC-138/STAR MAX/Ipx/AP Images
Interior Photos: Theo Wargo/Getty Images Entertainment/Getty Images, 4–5; Evan Agostini/Invision/AP Images, 8–9; Shutterstock Images, 11, 18, 20, 24–25, 28, 37, 38, 47, 58–59, 62–63, 71, 72–73, 76, 81; Astrid Stawiarz/Getty Images Entertainment/Getty Images, 12; Fabrice Dimier/Bloomberg/Getty Images, 15; Robyn Beck/AFP/Getty Images, 17; Wenn/AP Images, 22–23; Amanda Edwards/WireImage/Getty Images, 30; Randy Shropshire/Getty Images Entertainment/Getty Images, 34–35; Jeff Kravitz/FilmMagic/Getty Images, 40, 94–95, 97; Christopher Polk/Coachella/Getty Images Entertainment/Getty Images, 44–45; Robb Cohen/Invision/AP Images, 48–49; Jordan Strauss/Invision/AP Images, 51, 52; 352628Globe Photos/MediaPunch/IPX/AP Images, 55; Chris McKay/Getty Images Entertainment/Getty Images, 56; Xavier Collin/Image Press Agency/Sipa USA/AP Images, 64–65, 86–87; Charles Sykes/Invision/AP Images, 67; Press Association/URN:37417975/AP Images, 75; Emma McIntyre/The Recording Academy/Getty Images Entertainment/Getty Images, 78–79; Lester Cohen/The Recording Academy/Getty Images Entertainment/Getty Images, 90–91; Emerson Santos/Fotoarena/Sipa/AP Images, 93

Editor: Megan Ellis
Series Designer: Laura Graphenteen

LIBRARY OF CONGRESS CONTROL NUMBER: 2019941952

PUBLISHER'S CATALOGING-IN-PUBLICATION DATA

Names: Lusted, Marcia Amidon, author.
Title: Post Malone: rapper, singer, and songwriter / by Marcia Amidon Lusted
Other title: rapper, singer, and songwriter
Description: Minneapolis, Minnesota : Abdo Publishing, 2020 | Series: Hip-hop artists | Includes online resources and index.
Identifiers: ISBN 9781532190209 (lib. bdg.) | ISBN 9781532176050 (ebook)
Subjects: LCSH: Malone, Post, 1995- (Austin Post)--Juvenile literature. | Rap (Music) --Juvenile literature. | Songwriters--Juvenile literature. | Sound recording executives and producers--Juvenile literature. | Singers--Juvenile literature.
Classification: DDC 782.421649--dc23

CONTENTS

Chapter ONE

NEW AND OLD

On August 20, 2018, Radio City Music Hall in New York, New York, was filled with celebrities for the 2018 MTV Video Music Awards (VMAs). Nominees included artists such as Ariana Grande, Bruno Mars, Cardi B, Jennifer Lopez, and Childish Gambino. Many more musicians performed onstage during the awards show. Among them was hip-hop artist Post Malone, whose song featuring rapper 21 Savage, "Rockstar," won the Song of the Year. Post had also been nominated for Song of the Summer and Best Artist. At the end of the night, Post performed a lo-fi version of "Rockstar" wearing a white suit decorated with pink, yellow, and blue smiley faces. He danced and spun around an electric guitarist while white lights flashed in the dark theater. Soon, 21 Savage joined the performers onstage, and together they sang and rapped to a screaming crowd.

As "Rockstar" faded out, Post Malone grabbed an electric guitar from the side of the stage. "Ladies and gentlemen," he said, "it's f******* Aerosmith!"[1] The cameras

Post Malone received the Moon Person trophy for winning at the 2018 MTV Video Music Awards.

panned back and revealed the rock band Aerosmith on an elevated platform. The music faded in as front man Steven Tyler began singing the band's 1973 hit song "Dream On." Post danced around the stage and played his electric guitar through "Dream On" and then sang with Tyler and band member Joe Perry on another song, "Toys in the Attic."

The performance was high-energy and celebratory after Post's win, with Perry jamming his guitar into an amp as pyrotechnics shot up from the stage. Lights flashed and illuminated Post as he strummed his guitar. To close out the performance, Tyler put his arms around Perry and Post as all three shared one microphone. According to *Rolling Stone*, the "sacred mic-sharing" offered a "heartwarming sense of continuity," as Aerosmith had won a VMA for Video of the Year 25 years earlier.[2] Post hadn't even been born yet when Aerosmith

WHAT IS HIP-HOP?

Rap music is one part of hip-hop culture. Hip-hop includes deejaying (sometimes called turntabling), rap music itself, graffiti art, and B-boying, which is a style of dance as well as a fashion style, attitude, and type of body language. According to DJ KRS-One, who looks at the social theory of rap music, "Rap is something you do, hip-hop is something you live."[3]

had some of its biggest hits, but his excitement to perform with the group was clear. As the performance finished, Post wrapped his arms around Tyler in a hug from behind. He had a huge smile on his face.

WHO IS POST MALONE?

Post's appearance at the 2018 VMAs showed that the 23-year-old musician from Texas had already become a major presence in the world of hip-hop music. He was relatively new to creating music, yet he had become one of the most well-known hip-hop artists in the music business. However, Post has resisted having his music style placed into a specific

AEROSMITH

The band Aerosmith formed in Boston, Massachusetts, in 1970. It has had many top-selling albums and songs, despite problems with its members leaving and returning, as well as members battling drug addictions. Some of their most famous songs include "Dream On," "Sweet Emotion," and "I Don't Want to Miss a Thing." Working with hip-hop artists such as Post Malone is not new for the band. Aerosmith also collaborated with hip-hop band Run-D.M.C. in 1986. Together they remixed Aerosmith's song "Walk This Way." Many people said that the collaboration bridged the gap between hip-hop and rock music.

"As an artist, it's never really enough. You always wanna strive to get bigger and better and push the limits of what you can actually do."[4]

– Post Malone

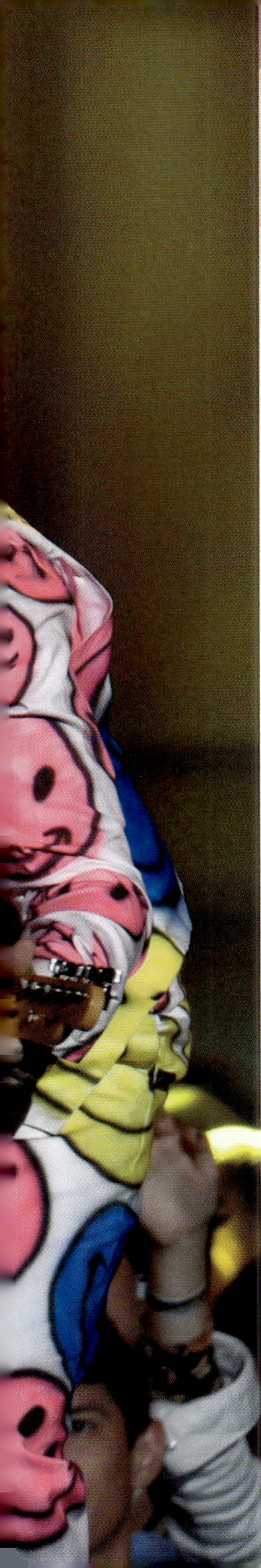

Post Malone, *right*, sang with Aerosmith on some of the band's most famous songs.

category, according to a 2018 interview with *GQ* magazine. The article spoke of Malone as "part of the new wave of rappers blurring the borders of hip-hop. [It's] pop, R&B, rap, emo, punk, and indie rock, thrown together in unpredictable and unpredictably compelling ways." Post said in the interview:

> *It should just be music, you know? Because I've met so many people that'll say, "I listen to everything except for this, or this," you know? And I think that's stupid. If you like it, you should listen to it.*[5]

Post's songs often combine elements from several musical genres. "White Iverson" combines emo, rap, and folk, and "Go Flex" has elements of country, R&B, and pop. Post constantly looks for ways to combine elements of other music in his own way and make his songs accessible to many different listeners. According to journalist Bijan Stephen in the *GQ* article, "Post is

Post Malone performs various styles of music from folk to rap.

trying to create bops for everyday use—morning jams that double as late-night music, that can fit every time in between."[6]

Post's musical flexibility has worked for him. In just a few years, he went from playing guitar in high school to appearing on music charts, singing with well-known hip-hop and rap artists, and having his records reach platinum sales levels. Platinum records have sold or streamed over one million units. To better understand his music, it's important to see how Austin Richard Post became Post Malone and how he became so famous so quickly.

EASY TO LIKE

According to Berklee College of Music songwriting professors Kareem Clarke and Brian "Raydar" Ellis in an interview with *Vice*, Post Malone's music is a success because of its structure. Ellis noted how this structure worked in the song "Rockstar": "We've got a lot of sixteenth note rhythms that'll maybe repeat for three times and then go into a nice ending phrase. . . . It makes it easier for the normal listener to latch on to that and remember it and know what's about to come next."[7]

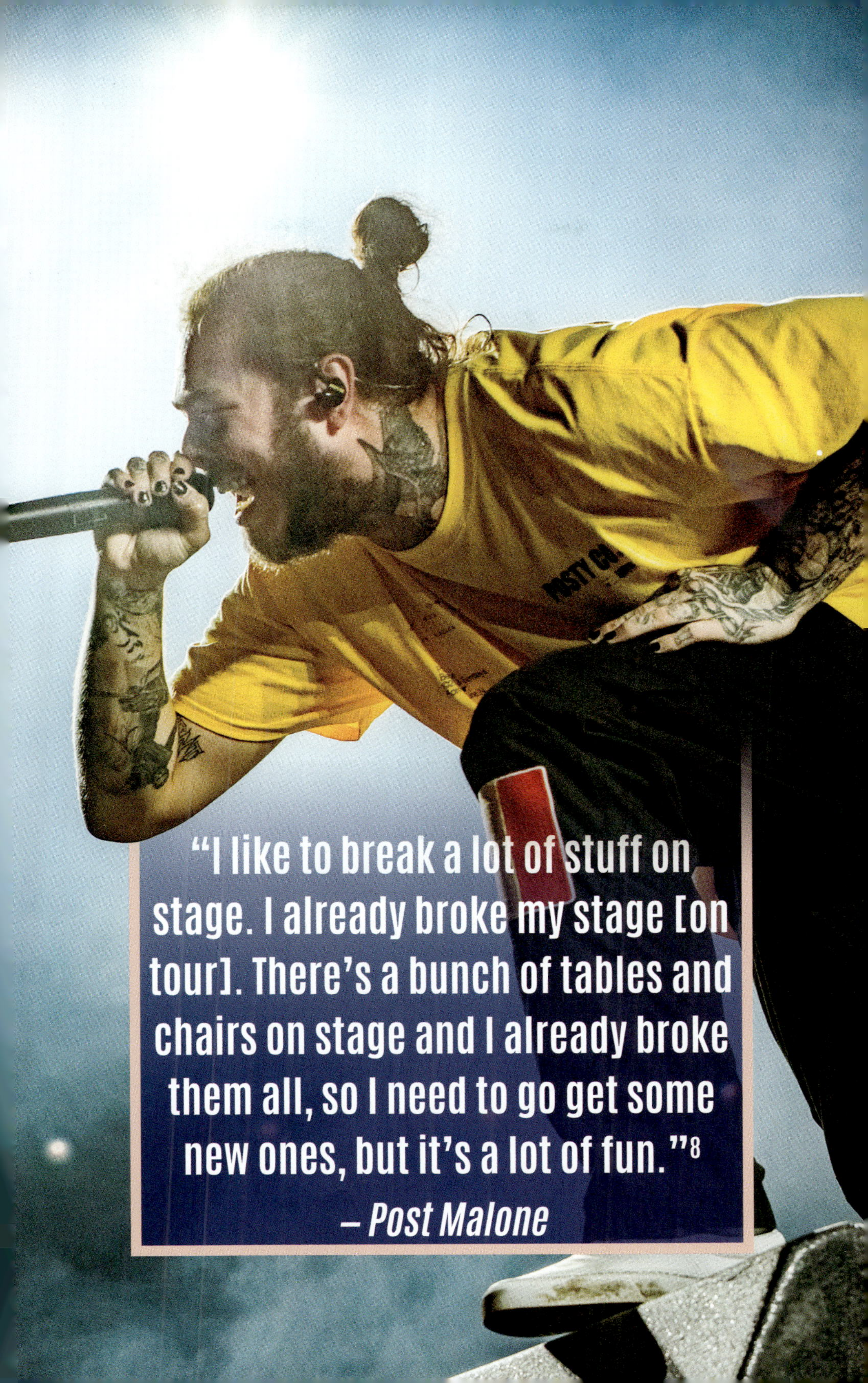

"I like to break a lot of stuff on stage. I already broke my stage [on tour]. There's a bunch of tables and chairs on stage and I already broke them all, so I need to go get some new ones, but it's a lot of fun."[8]

– Post Malone

Chapter TWO

BECOMING POST

Austin Richard Post was born in Syracuse, New York, on July 4, 1995. His family had Italian roots, as his grandfather on his mother's side had Italian parents. Post says he has Native American ancestry as well. He was raised by his father, Rich Post, and his stepmother, Jodie. Rich and Jodie met when they were both working for an industrial laundry company in Syracuse. Both Rich and Jodie had children from previous relationships—Rich had Austin, and Jodie had a son, Mitchell. Austin enjoyed going to the New York State Fair every summer with his family, playing video games, and hanging out with his friends.

Austin's father had once been a disc jockey for a company called Whirlin' Disc DJs, which supplied music for weddings. Rich was used to playing a wide variety of music, from country to hip-hop and classic rock, depending on what the wedding couples wanted. Rich had also been to many concerts in the Syracuse area, seeing acts like Mötley Crüe, Twisted Sister,

Post Malone has had many different fashion and hair styles over the years.

Bruce Springsteen, and Billy Idol. "I was a heavy metal, hair band kind of guy," Rich said.[1]

Because of his father's wide-ranging musical tastes, Austin was introduced to many different types of music, each of which would eventually influence his own songwriting. "My dad was always playing music," Austin later said. "Not like playing music, but listening to music. And he put me on everything . . . folk and funk and rap. . . . And from then on I just started making what I like. . . . And just making music."[2]

CELEBRITIES FROM GRAPEVINE

Post Malone is not the only celebrity from Grapevine, Texas. Norah Jones is a singer-songwriter who has won nine Grammy awards throughout her career. She even attended the same high school as Post, Grapevine High School, many years before he did. Jones credits her childhood in Grapevine as largely influential to her music. Dancer and actress Jenna Dewan also attended Grapevine High School. She was a varsity cheerleader before dancing in music videos for artists such as Janet Jackson and Ricky Martin. She also starred in the 2006 movie *Step Up*.

FROM NEW YORK TO TEXAS

Austin and his family moved to Grapevine, Texas, when he was nine. Grapevine is about 20 miles (32 km) northwest of Dallas, Texas. Austin's father had gotten a new job as the manager of food and beverage concessions at AT&T Stadium, home of the Dallas Cowboys football team. In Grapevine, Austin developed his passion for music. When he was 12 years old, he began playing *Guitar Hero*. The video game inspired him to learn to play a real guitar. He said, "It got to a point where on expert, you can only exceed to a certain point. And so you know, I was like let's play real guitar. Let's not waste more time."[3]

His mother bought him a Washburn Lyon guitar for Christmas. But it wasn't easy to go from playing *Guitar*

***Guitar Hero* controllers have buttons on the neck instead of strings. They connect to video game consoles.**

Post Malone played guitar during his performance at the 2019 Grammy Awards.

A TEACHER REMEMBERS POST

Jared Miller, Austin's middle school geometry teacher, recalled having him in his class. "[Austin] always had good grades," Miller said. "He laughed at others' jokes but he never made a lot himself." Miller commented that he didn't see any indication of a musical talent in him at the time, saying, "[Austin] really liked *Guitar Hero*, but everyone did, it was a big game then."[6]

Hero to a real guitar. Austin said, "The transition was awful. . . . You feel cool as h*** with the [*Guitar Hero*] guitar in your hand, but it is not the same at all."[4] Austin also watched YouTube videos of bands such as Metallica and AC/DC to help him learn how to play. His father offered to pay for guitar lessons, but after six months of playing, according to his father, Austin said, "Nope, I developed my own style."[5]

> **"[Learning to play guitar] took a long time, because I used to suck. I was really bad. . . . You just gotta stick with it, because a lot of people wanna give up whenever they first start something."[7]**
>
> *– Post Malone*

PERFORMING AND AUDITIONING

When Austin was in the eighth grade in 2008, he received his first taste of musical success at a talent

contest. He won it with a metalcore cover of Rihanna's "Umbrella." Metalcore is a musical genre that combines punk and metal sounds. In 2010, when he was 15 years old, Austin auditioned for the metalcore band Crown the Empire, which was forming in Dallas at the time.

Rihanna's music inspired a young Post Malone.

However, he was rejected after his guitar strings broke during his audition. But after that experience, Austin kept working on his performances. Rich recalled, "We'd drive him all over the place anyplace that would let him play. Open mike nights, where he'd do covers of Guns N' Roses and Outkast."[8]

CHICKEN EXPRESS

When he was a teenager, Austin had a part-time job working for Chicken Express, a fast-food chain in the southern United States. In 2018, Malone took a film crew into Chicken Express as part of a documentary about his life. In the segment, Post says, "I worked here because I was trying to make some money so I could buy some Versace shoes."[9] He says that he spent all of the $800 he saved from the job on those shoes.

When he was in high school, Austin started sharing his music on a streaming site called SoundCloud. SoundCloud is a website for distributing audio and sharing music. It lets users upload, promote, and share their audio files. Post's old SoundCloud account, under the name Austin Richard, included a guitar version of the Christmas song "Silent Night," as well as an original song called "Stairs and Strangers."

In high school, Austin also recorded his first mixtape, called *Young and After Them Riches*. He shared the mixtape

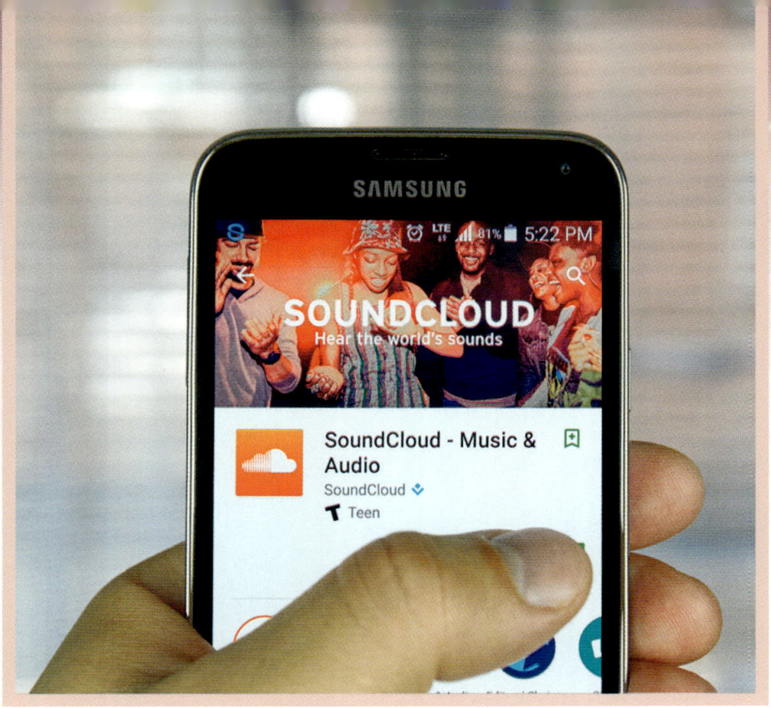

SoundCloud is available as an app for iPhone and Android smartphones.

with people at his school, and when he was a senior, his classmates voted him "Most Likely to Become Famous." Post Malone later said:

> *When I was 16, I started recording my own mixtape . . . and I thought it was fire. I was like, This s*** is so hard, and everybody at school was like, "Yeah bro, this s*** is hard." In retrospect, it was awful. My beats were hard, but I sucked. I had no identity or anything, I was 16.*[10]

While Austin was in high school, he created an alter ego character named Leon DeChino for a school art project. As DeChino, he recorded a humorous synth-pop song and video called "Why Don't You Love Me?" In the video, Austin is wearing tights and doing a silly dance with a friend. The character of Leon DeChino would later be referenced in Post Malone's video for the song "Psycho."

FROM AUSTIN POST TO POST MALONE

How did Post Malone get his stage name? Austin came up with the name Post Malone when he was 14 or 15. In an interview with Jimmy Fallon on *The Tonight Show*, Post claims that he used an online rap name generator to come up with the name "Malone." It is also rumored that he chose Malone as a reference to the professional basketball player Karl Malone.

In 2013, Austin Post, who by then had already created his rapper name of Post Malone, graduated from high school in Grapevine. While he planned to attend college in the fall, he had also taken the first steps to start a music career. His musical ambition ended up changing his plans. Post describes himself as someone who is very dedicated to making music because he has a lot of ambition. He stated that he is "always grinding, always working, always tired, but . . . staying up, anyway."[11]

POSTY

Chapter THREE

LEAVING FOR LOS ANGELES

By the end of high school, Post Malone had taught himself how to play the guitar as well as how to use sound editing software such as Audacity and FL Studios. However, he didn't have enough money to take classes or hire private teachers. Post later told *HuffPost* that without money, making music professionally is "so out of your reach, it's so out of your grasp. It's just tough to find a way that you can get a medium of yourself out there."[1] At the same time, he was in four different bands and struggling to find his own sound and his own musical style.

Post enrolled at Tarrant County College near Dallas, Texas, with the goal of becoming a musician. But he didn't last long. "Yeah, I dropped out of there," he said on Twitter. "I wasn't very good at school. And I moved to L.A. like a real cool, punk kid."[2]

Post Malone's music career took off after he moved to Los Angeles, California.

The Encino neighborhood is located in the San Fernando Valley.

HEADING FOR LA

Post decided that if he wanted to seriously pursue a music career, he needed to leave Texas and move to California. His best friend, Jason Probst, was also interested in leaving Texas. Probst was a *Minecraft* streamer on YouTube, and Post would sometimes appear in Probst's videos. The friends decided to move to Los Angeles together.

Probst rented an apartment in Los Angeles, and Post moved in with him rent free. He lived in Probst's closet so the bedroom could be turned into a music studio.

He and Probst met Billie Gvtes—a Los Angeles producer, skateboarder, rapper, and songwriter—as well as some other music producers and performers. Together, they formed the music group BLKCVRD.

Several members of BLKCVRD moved into a mansion in the Encino neighborhood of Los Angeles. They called it the White House and referred to it as a

> **"Make music that you love. Don't listen to what nobody says. You're gonna do good. You're gonna be proud of yourself if you just keep on rocking."[3]**
>
> ***–Post Malone***

"multimedia mansion."[4] Post met songwriter and music producer Trocon Markous Roberts Jr., also known as FKi 1st. FKi 1st joined BLKCVRD. He collaborated with Post in the White House, where they would play and write music together.

FKI 1ST

Producer and musician Trocon Markous Roberts Jr., known as FKi 1st, credits his interest in music production to the summer after his freshman year of high school. "I was in trouble with my parents because I did horrible in my classes," he said in an interview. "So I couldn't go anywhere that summer. . . . A friend showed me how to make beats. I thought, 'Yeah, I can do this.'"[5] FKi 1st has since produced fifteen gold and platinum records by artists such as 2 Chainz, Travis Porter, and Post Malone, and he also recorded his own solo EP, *First Time for Everything*.

"WHITE IVERSON"

Post would soon write his first hit song, "White Iverson," while living in Encino. Post says that "White Iverson" is named partly because of basketball player Allen Iverson, who played 17 seasons in the NBA. When Post braided his own hair much like Iverson's, he came up with the "White Iverson"

> **"There's a lot of recycled bulls*** out there. Almost the majority of it is just the same song over and over again. I think it's time for a change. We need to turn up on 'em. Real quick."[6]**
>
> *–Post Malone*

title because he thought he looked like a white version of the African American athlete. The song is also filled with basketball references, including players Michael Jordan, Shaquille O'Neal, and James Harden.

He wrote the first verse of the song, but then set it aside for a few days. Then, Post said, "I woke up a couple of days later, and had to finish it, cause I was like, 'I wanted to put this out. This song is dope.'"

Post decided to record the song and asked for help from his frequent collaborator and producer Rex Kudo. Kudo taught Post how to use the music software Logic. Post recalls thinking, "Are people gonna like this? That's the first time I really ever made a track like that. . . . [Kudo] was like, '. . . I'm gonna record this. This is fire.'"[7]

LOGIC

Post Malone used Logic to create his song "White Iverson." Logic Pro X is a music production software created by Apple. Artists can import their own music and add sound clips, or "loops," to the tracks. These loops layer together to create songs with multiple instruments. There are more than 7,000 loops in Logic Pro X for various instruments from synthesizers to drums. Logic also helps artists maintain a consistent tempo and pitch. These tools make it easier for both amateurs and professionals to create music digitally.

Reebok Reebok Reebok

Allen Iverson, *right*, played the shooting guard and point guard positions in basketball.

Fans agreed with Post. According to him, "I just put ["White Iverson"] out and went about my life and I woke up the next morning . . . and [it] was wild."[8] The song was an overnight hit. "White Iverson" received more than two million plays in its first month online. The success of "White Iverson" put Post in the spotlight as a successful hip-hop artist. It was his first taste of success, as well as his first experience of criticism. Many music critics felt he would be a one-hit wonder and unable to come up with another hit song. But Post was only getting started.

ACOUSTIC MALONE

Despite his success as a rapper, Post wants his fans to see that he writes and sings other types of music as well. He has recorded a cover of Bob Dylan's folk rock song "Don't Think Twice, It's All Right," and he has said that he is working on some more acoustic music. According to Post, acoustic music "has a really cool vibe and I think it's a really important vibe for music. I think we need something like that."[9]

CLIMBING THE LADDER

Chapter FOUR

Much of the success of "White Iverson" was due to the hard work of Post and his manager, Dre London. London met Post Malone in 2014 when he visited Malone's house in Encino. London saw a lot of potential in the gamers, artists, and producers living there, but he was really focusing on just one person: Post Malone. London moved into the house and found himself managing Post Malone when his "White Iverson" climbed the music charts.

London and Post had to push back against the assumption that Post would be a one-hit wonder. *Billboard* magazine asked London how difficult it was to convince people that Post was more than just one song. According to London, "Really, all I had to do was . . . keep screaming about how he was the next best thing in the world. . . . People looked over and they saw a white guy

Post's career took off after the release of "White Iverson."

with Allen Iverson cornrows and gold teeth, and they didn't take me serious."[1]

London and Post worked to get the song everywhere on the internet, as well as in music clubs, which then led to it being played on the radio. "It was fighting for each crumb," London said. "We just had a hunch and we had a vibe and knew that something [about Post's music] was totally different."[2]

"I'm trying my best here. That's all I can do."[3]
– Post Malone, via Twitter

A NEW LOOK

Following the release of "White Iverson," Post wore his hair braided into cornrows, similar to the ones worn by Allen Iverson. Cornrows are a hairstyle that emerged in Africa in 3,000 BCE. Some news outlets look down on this hairstyle when sported by black people but praise it for being edgy and chic when worn by white celebrities such as Post Malone, Cara Delavigne, and Natalie Dormer.

Many people feel that white people with cornrows are appropriating black culture. When asked if he expected to be criticized for his look, Post replied, "It's not normal for a white guy to get cornrows; a lot of people judged me. I like the way it looks, so you have to be confident. If you like something, rock it."[4]

REPUBLIC RECORDS

"White Iverson" debuted in February 2015 and Post Malone signed with Republic Records that August. He hadn't even recorded a full-length album yet. Post said he had multiple offers from many different record labels, but ultimately he chose Republic. According to Post, "I think I just knew automatically . . . so that's where I wanted to go."[5]

Once Post signed with Republic, the company rereleased "White Iverson." The song debuted at Number 84 on the *Billboard* Hot 100 chart and reached Number 14. As of 2019, "White Iverson" was certified 5x platinum. This means it had sold or streamed five million units. Post also released several more songs on SoundCloud, including "Holyfield" and "What's Up."

REPUBLIC RECORDS

Brothers Monte and Avery Lipman founded Republic Records in 1995. In 2000, Universal Music Group acquired the label. Republic Records has signed many famous artists over the years, including Post Malone, Ariana Grande, Hailee Steinfeld, and Stevie Wonder. In 2018, Republic Records was named the top label by *Billboard*. It also was the *Billboard* Hot 100 top label every year from 2014 to 2018.

Not every critic liked "White Iverson," however. In an article for the music publication *Pitchfork*, contributor Matthew Ramirez said that though the song was "charming" and had "a certain nostalgic desire and childlike wonder," it was only a one-hit wonder. While discussing Post's

Post takes time to connect with his fans during his concerts.

first album, Ramirez continued, "Even if you liked 'White Iverson,' was there anyone who thought to themselves, *I want to hear this guy's story! What's he all about? We need to know more!?*"[6]

Post also received criticism because he would play "White Iverson" twice during each of his concerts. He would open and close the show with the same song. Post argued that this was because he did not have very many songs to perform. He stated, "I only had one good song. I still only have one good song, but I had to do ["White Iverson"] first and I had to do it last 'cause no one knew who . . . I was."[7]

However, soon Post began working with many well-known rappers, such as 50 Cent and Young Thug. Post headlined a show in Dallas in 2015 and then received an invitation later that year to perform at reality star and business mogul Kylie Jenner's eighteenth birthday party.

At the party, Malone met rapper, singer, producer, entrepreneur, and fashion designer Kanye West. West's music is known for changing styles and incorporating many different influences, ranging from synth-pop to indie rock, electro, and gospel. According to Post, West liked Post's music and the two of them ended up in the studio together. He added,

BILLBOARD CHARTS

Billboard magazine is best known for the series of charts it publishes ranking the popularity of albums and songs in different genres of music. They base their popularity ratings on downloads, album and song sales, radio airplay, and social media interactions and streaming. Categories include the Hot 100, *Billboard* 200, and Artist 100, as well as charts in individual music genres such as Rock Songs, R&B/Hip-Hop Songs, and Country Songs.

Kanye West frequently collaborates with other artists, including Post Malone.

> *[Kanye West] sent me a session . . . and when I went back to Los Angeles we got into the studio together. . . . It was the scariest experience ever. Letting him listen to you record . . . it's intimidating, but he is such a cool guy.*[8]

As Post's songs climbed higher on the *Billboard* charts, his popularity grew with fans around the world.

The song collaboration between West and Malone, titled "Fade," also featured rapper Ty Dolla $ign. Post's verse included the lines "I've been so led on, I've been runnin' 'round."[9] According to Post, the lyrics were about how people were critical of his rise to fame. He said, "I don't know if [the critiques are] because I am white or because I am young or because I came up really fast or whatever."[10]

TY DOLLA $IGN

Ty Dolla $ign is a rapper from Los Angeles, California. In addition to collaborating with Post Malone on Kanye West's "Fade," the two also worked together on "Psycho," which topped the *Billboard* Hot 100 in 2018. Ty Dolla $ign has worked with many artists, including Fifth Harmony, YG, Skrillex, and Jason Derulo. In 2019, he released the album MihTy with rapper Jeremih.

"Fade" was released on West's album *The Life of Pablo* in February 2016 and reached Number 47 on the *Billboard* Hot 100 list. Post was successfully fighting the label of one-hit wonder as his music became more and more popular. His presence in pop culture and in music would only continue to grow.

Chapter FIVE

OUT IN THE WORLD

On March 8, 2016, singer Justin Bieber announced that Post would be one of the opening acts on the North American segment of Bieber's Purpose World Tour. Even with the success Post had already had, many people really didn't know who he was. They wondered just who this young white rapper from Texas was, and why Bieber had chosen him.

Bieber and Post met in Los Angeles when a mutual friend introduced them, and they became friends. They even recorded in the studio together. As Malone said, "[We] made a couple great jams together. Then [Bieber] said, 'Come on tour with me,' and ain't no way you're going to say 'no' to the Purpose Tour."[1]

Though Post is now known for having many tattoos, he didn't get his first tattoo until touring with Justin Bieber. Bieber is also known for his many tattoos.

The Purpose World Tour exposed Post to fans who might not have otherwise listened to his music.

THE PURPOSE WORLD TOUR

Post Malone joined Justin Bieber for some of the Purpose World Tour dates in North America. However, the tour also traveled to Australia and countries in South America, Asia, Europe, and Africa between March 2016 and July 2017. On July 24, 2017, Bieber announced that he would cancel the final 14 shows on the tour. People speculated that this was due to the rigorous and exhausting tour schedule. Over the 17 months of the tour, which was the fifth-largest tour of 2016, Bieber performed 150 shows. In his announcement, Bieber stated that he was excited to take some time for "just resting, getting some relaxation."[3]

According to Post, "We were working on [the album] Stoney, and then we had a tattoo artist come through, and I was like, 'You know what? Justin Bieber's got some tats, and I love you, but I know I'm way tougher than [Bieber].'"

However, Post also blames Bieber for what happened after his first tattoo. A few days later, as he and Bieber were playing basketball, Bieber accidentally bumped into Post and scraped the scab off the still-healing tattoo. According to Post, "[He] knocked the whole thing off. It was just blood dripping down my hand."[2] Post says that the injury affected the look of his

"Bieber's like my brother at this point. We've been through a lot of stuff together already. . . . He's always been so supportive and I'm there to support him."[4]

–Post Malone

tattoo, but he appreciates the story behind how it looks.

Bieber had also released Instagram photos of him and Post hanging out and roughhousing, with captions such as "Go bestfriend that's my bestfriend" and "Silly people's."[5] After a photo surfaced that appeared to show Post choking Bieber after Bieber put a cigarette out on his arm, Post commented, saying that the fight wasn't real: "He's my big brother and we like to rough house . . . if we was fighting someone would have done something instead of just sit around while [Bieber] gets

"DON'T TREAD ON ME"

One of Post Malone's tattoos is of a snake curled around an M16 rifle. The snake is the same one that appears on the "Don't Tread on Me" flag, a historical flag from the Revolutionary War. It symbolized the American colonists' desire for independence and their refusal to be taken advantage of by Britain. Later, the symbol became associated with people who want to protect the Second Amendment, or the right to bear arms.

"Your [*sic*] a beautiful person Posty! . . . Truly an honor to know you my brother!"[7]

– *Justin Bieber*

Bieber, *right*, and Post remained friends after finishing the Purpose World Tour.

chokeslammed."[6] Shortly after, Bieber posted a photo in which he appeared to be choking Post.

The Purpose World Tour started on March 9, 2016. Post remained with the tour until July 2016, when Bieber

left for other tour dates around the world. Touring was a new experience for Post. He was used to playing in small venues. Suddenly, he was performing in large arenas with huge stages. The tour also exposed Post to a new

> **"I am in this for the pure purpose of creating what I want, because it's who I am."[9]**
>
> ***–Post Malone***

audience, younger than his usual base of fans. Often, there were middle school kids with their parents. But Post received a good reception from Bieber's audiences. He said, "Even the younger kids have been into it; the parents have been into it; no one has been very upset with me."[8]

POST, BIEBER, AND RELIGION

In 2017, Post said in a *Rolling Stone* interview that his friend Justin Bieber had donated $10 million to Hillsong, a megachurch that is popular with celebrities. Malone mentioned that Bieber had gotten very religious. Though Post said he also believed in God, he thought that large donations like Bieber's were unnecessary. He added, "It's nice to support something you believe in, I guess, but people are spending so much money, and God doesn't care that your church has a . . . gold roof."[10]

JIMMY KIMMEL LIVE!

Even while he was touring with Justin Bieber, Post was still working on his own music. In June 2016, he appeared on the television show *Jimmy Kimmel Live!* and performed his newest hit single, "Go Flex." It had been released on April 21, 2016, on the Beats 1 radio station. Post talked about the song with radio host DJ Zane Lowe, saying, "It's a little

Jimmy Kimmel is a producer and late-night television host.

bit of everything that I love. . . . It just happened to come together really cool."[11] The version that he performed on *Jimmy Kimmel Live!* was different, however. Post replaced the original synthesizer and drum machine with a guitar, while the rhythm of the song was more of a straight rock and roll beat. This version of the song received mixed reviews from his fans, who were confused as to what genre of music Malone was really playing.

Quavo, *right*, is part of the rap group Migos along with family members Offset, *left*, and Takeoff, *center*.

In addition to "Go Flex," Malone also released his first mixtape, *August 26*, on May 12, 2016. The title was a promotion for Malone's first album, which would be released on August 26, 2016. The mixtape included guest performances by artists Jaden Smith, Lil Yachty, Jeremih, 2 Chainz, and Trae tha Truth.

On August 26, 2016, Malone released his first album with Republic Records, *Stoney*. As with his mixtape, the album had guest appearances by many well-known artists, including Justin Bieber, Quavo, and Kehlani. *Stoney* received mixed reviews. In a review for *Pitchfork*, Matthew Ramirez stated, "Post Malone

Post Malone's album *Stoney* contained a variety of different musical genres and styles.

releases a 68-minute album that shows exactly why he should have never been given the chance to release a 68-minute album."[12] However, in a review on the amateur music-review website Sputnikmusic, a listener said that the album "showcases an artist with a sound so catchy yet varied, but with plenty of room to grow as both a person and as a musician."[13]

Stoney peaked at Number 4 on the US *Billboard* 200 chart. After four months, the album went platinum and spent three weeks in the Number 1 position on the R&B/Hip-Hop Albums chart. It would eventually remain in the Top 10 for 77 weeks, breaking the chart record of 76 weeks set by Michael Jackson's 1982 album *Thriller*.

XXL FRESHMEN

XXL, a US hip-hop magazine, publishes an annual "Freshman Class" list of ten artists they think people should notice and watch for. Some are new artists, while others are underground performers that the magazine has taken notice of. The ten freshmen appear on the magazine's cover, which gives them publicity. When *XXL*'s editor in chief, Vanessa Satten, was asked why Post Malone was not included in the 2016 freshman list, she stated that she had been told by Malone's team that he was starting to move away from the hip-hop genre.

However, Malone later insisted that he is not leaving hip-hop behind. He added, "I want to continue to work with talented artists across any genre, and continue doing the s*** that I love."[14]

Ludwig

Chapter SIX

ALBUMS, INTERVIEWS, AND ACCIDENTS

In a November 2017 interview with Polish media outlet *NewOnce*, Post stated that people who want to listen to meaningful music should not listen to hip-hop because the lyrics aren't as real as those in other music. He said "If you're looking to cry, if you're looking to think about life, don't listen to hip-hop. . . . Whenever I want to sit down and have a nice cry, I'll listen to some Bob Dylan." Post added that he listens to hip-hop when he's "trying to have a good time and stay in a positive mood. . . . I think hip-hop . . . brings people together in a beautiful, happy way."[1]

Immediately, people took offense at Post's comments. Hip-hop fans were angry that Malone was insulting the genre that had brought him fame. He had already been

People have accused Post of being a "culture vulture" because he wins awards for his hip-hop music but hesitates to call himself a hip-hop artist.

"I have not had all the life experience in the world to talk about the most meaningful s*. I just sing about what I have gone through, what's going on in my life, and what I wanna sing about."[4]**

– Post Malone

LIL B

Lil B, also known as The BasedGod, is a rapper from California. He became famous through viral posts and commentary on social media. Though Lil B has not won any awards, he has almost 1.4 million followers on Twitter. He is also known for his prolific songwriting, releasing many new songs every year. By April 2012, he claimed to have released more than 2,000 songs. He has released several albums and dozens of mixtapes, including one mixtape with more than 676 songs.[5] As of 2019, his only charting album was *I'm Gay* (2011), which peaked at Number 56 on the *Billboard* charts.

accused in the past of using hip-hop culture to his own advantage. Other hip-hop artists, producers, and directors chimed in, too. Rapper Vince Stales said on Snapchat, "Somebody go tell Post Malone to listen to Future's verse on '3500.' If he can't cry to that I don't know what to tell him."[2] Director Xavier Burgin, known on Twitter as XLNB, stated, "Hip Hop is both communal and divisive, spiritual & emotionally poignant. The idea you need to listen to Bob Dylan to 'cry' is ludicrous as is the idea hip hop is a mechanism purely to make 'everyone happy.'"[3]

Rapper and activist Lil B had already made his

Bob Dylan is a singer-songwriter who has toured for over 50 years.

opinion of Post Malone clear in a series of tweets before Malone's *NewOnce* interview. Lil B was upset about Post's change in music genre. In October 2017, he said, "Give it a few years [Post Malone] be full country and hate blacks lol - Lil B." The two engaged in a series of back-and-forth tweets, and included critical comments about Post making "fake hip hop country music." Lil B added, "Post Malone just mad cuz I no he make country western music not hip hop it's ok brother! We support u anyway!!! U platinum! Good job."[6]

Post Malone responded to all the criticism that followed his interview, claiming that it was partly due to the fact that he was intoxicated at the time. He said,

Lil B also raps as his alter ego The BasedGod.

"Who the f*** am I to tell you don't listen to this and whenever you wanna feel something don't listen to this? Or who am I to tell you that you should feel a certain way when listening to something?" Fellow rapper Logic also supported Post. He tweeted, "That's my homie! Good dude great artist and all around gentleman."[7]

NEW MUSIC

While the controversy over the *NewOnce* interview was still raging, Post was getting ready to release a new album, *Beerbongs & Bentleys*. Two singles from the album were previewed before its release. The song

"WE KNEW THE SONG WAS GREAT"

Lorenzo Cardona, a recording engineer at Quad Recording Studios in New York City, described what it was like to work on Post Malone's song "Rockstar," the lead single from *Beerbongs & Bentleys*. He said, "When we were in the studio . . . we knew the song was great, but we didn't know how far the song would go." Cardona added that Post did not think the song would be more popular than "White Iverson." However, Cardona said that "sometimes the stars are aligned in the universe." "Rockstar" was destined to be a huge hit.[8]

"[*Beerbongs & Bentleys*] is such a broad span of music and I think it all comes together in such a weird perfect way that I think it's going to be one of the best records of the year."[9]

– Post Malone, September 2017

Like Post Malone, Ty Dolla $ign raps and plays instruments.

"Rockstar," featuring 21 Savage, debuted in September 2017 as the album's lead single. "Psycho," which featured Ty Dolla $ign, was released on February 21, 2018, debuting at Number 2 and peaking at Number 1 on the *Billboard* Hot 100 chart. The full album came out in April 2018.

Beerbongs & Bentleys broke the record for number of streams in a single week and debuted at Number 1 on the *Billboard* 200 Albums chart. The total number of streams from all tracks on the album reached 431 million, breaking the previous record of 385 million held by Drake for his 2017 album *More Life*. The album had the best sales week on the chart since Taylor Swift's 2017 album *Reputation*. Malone broke the record for having the most songs in the top 20 of the *Billboard* Hot 100 chart, with nine. The Beatles and J. Cole held the previous record of six.

As with Post's previous album, reviews of the album were mixed. *Rolling Stone*

> **"[Post Malone has] got a lot of country in him. He knows so much about country music, hip hop, rap, soul, blues, just everything. It's incredible."[12]**
> ***–Keith Urban, country musician***

MALONE AND MARIACHIS

In 2017, Post Malone was playing a concert as part of the Rolling Loud Festival in Miami, Florida. Dre London secretly hired a mariachi band through Postmates, a delivery service, to perform Post's hit song "Congratulations." London wanted to get Post excited and energized before his concert, but also work in some marketing for his album. Post made a video of the mariachi band's performance, and it went viral. In an interview with *Billboard*, London said, "All of a sudden, guess what? 'Congratulations' started hitting Mexico charts. I was seeing the impact of how to hit certain things. But it has to be genuine—you can't fake it."[13]

called it a "flexing, partying, rich-sad bummer."[10] *Billboard* magazine said, "[Post] understands the little bits of phrasing that turn memorable choruses into absolute brain infestations."[11] Despite mixed reviews, the album sold and sold throughout the year.

"GOD MUST HATE ME LOL"

Even though Post now had a string of hit songs and albums, as well as the lifestyle of a famous hip-hop artist, he had a series of unfortunate accidents and other incidents in 2018. On August 21, two of the tires on Post's private plane exploded on takeoff. The pilot was forced to keep the plane in the air for hours and burn off fuel before he attempted a dangerous landing with two flat tires. No one was injured, and the plane landed safely. Post later tweeted, "I landed guys. thank you for your prayers."[14] A little more than two weeks later, on September 7, in the early hours of the morning, the Rolls Royce that Post was riding in was struck by another car. The Rolls Royce went off the road and crashed into a fence. Again, fortunately, no one was injured. After the crash, Post tweeted, "god must hate me lol." He later added, "Ya can't kill me muthaf*****!"[15]

Then, three days after the car accident, Malone's former house was broken into. Three men, brandishing guns, smashed a window

"JUST GET IT OVER WITH"

In an interview with *Billboard* after the incident on his private plane, Post discussed his fear of flying as well as how he tried to remain calm during the event. He said that he normally tries to fall asleep on planes to combat his fear, but he was wide awake on this flight. Post continued, "We heard a big a** pop . . . and then s*** started coming in from underneath the table."

Post said that it was hard to trust that everything would be okay as the plane circled for hours to burn off fuel. "You figured if something is gonna happen, just get it over with, like a Band-Aid or something," he said. "S*** was scary! . . . But, we made it!"[16]

Post often raps about luxury cars such as Bentleys.

in the Encino house and yelled, asking for Post Malone. They hit one of the residents with their pistols. However, Malone had not lived in the house for a long time, and the people currently living there had no relationship to him. The men took about $20,000 worth of jewelry, cash,

and cell phones. The invasion seemed to have been part of a string of robberies hitting celebrities in the area in prior weeks. Even with the unfortunate accidents and incidents, Post continued to make music that defied genre classifications in 2018.

Chapter SEVEN

HIP-HOP AND HOLLYWOOD

On October 2, 2018, Post appeared on NBC's *The Tonight Show Starring Jimmy Fallon*. During the show, Post previewed a ten-second-long audio excerpt of a new song, "Sunflower," from the soundtrack to the animated movie *Spider-Man: Into the Spider-Verse*, which would come out in December 2018. The tiny portion of the song included Post singing "You're a sunflower / I think your love would be too much" over an accompaniment of drums and synthesizer.[1]

Post also joked with Fallon about how he celebrated everything by going to Olive Garden, a chain Italian restaurant. "From going platinum to going undefeated . . . in beer pong that night, we stay up and hit Olive Garden and celebrate right," Malone said.[2] According to Fallon, later:

Post typically wears eccentric clothing when he walks the red carpet at awards shows.

Fallon has hosted *The Tonight Show* since 2014.

He kept talking about how he loves the Olive Garden. I was like, "You keep saying this, but I've got to be honest, I've never been to an Olive Garden." He was like, "Are you kidding me? That really saddens me." I'm like, "Dude, I live in New York City. I'm not going to go to Olive Garden." He goes, "I'll take you there tonight." I go, "OK, if you want to; I'll go to the Olive Garden."[3]

The two men rode in Post's bright-pink stretch Hummer limo to the Olive Garden in Times Square and ate dinner, with many hilarious incidents over their wine and food. When Post Malone asked for a "laundry basket of croutons" with the salad, Fallon emerged from the kitchen with an actual laundry basket of the toasted bread. "You're the best dad ever," Post told Fallon.[4]

A NEW LOOK

In 2018, Post made a big change to his appearance: cutting off his hair. Post had always had either long, braided hair or loose shoulder-length hair. On the Instagram post debuting his new short, curly hair, he wrote, "plz don't stop listening to my music."[5] Some people speculated that his appearance change was for his role in an upcoming movie. Others thought it was just Post's latest way of changing up his style.

100

"In a hundred million years I would never expect to do this [win an award at the 2018 VMAs] ever. So this is sick, and thank you so much."[7]

– Post Malone

IRISH ENTERTAINMENT

When Post Malone and Jimmy Fallon visited Paddy Reilly's Music Bar, an Irish pub in New York City, it wasn't the first time that Malone showed his Irish singing abilities. On tour in Dublin, Ireland, in early 2018, he surprised his fans there by performing the Irish song "The Auld Triangle." After the Paddy Reilly's visit, the pub said on Facebook, "Delighted, honored, and privileged, to have a couple of locals in the House last night. Thanks to Jimmy Fallon and Post Malone for dropping in."[8]

After recording their meal for a segment on the show, Fallon began to head home, but Post wanted to stay out and party more. The two went to an Irish pub and jammed with other musicians and patrons. Video from the pub shows Fallon and Post singing with the crowd. Fallon later said that his voice was "still rough" many days after the experience.[6]

AWARDS, FESTIVALS, AND MOVIES

Post received many awards and nominations in 2018. After his win and performance at the 2018 VMAs, Post was nominated in six categories at the American Music Awards, including Artist of the Year. He won the awards Favorite Male Artist Pop/Rock and Favorite Hip-Hop Album for *Beerbongs & Bentleys*. His acceptance speech was simply, "I'm not very good at talking in front of people, but I just want to say thank you for the award, and I love you guys very very much."[9] However, while many people were excited about Post's win, others criticized him for his performance of "Psycho" with Ty Dolla $ign. Fans accused him of lip-synching to the song and not even doing a very good job of it.

In October 2018, Post inaugurated a new all-day hip-hop festival in Dallas called the Posty Fest.

"[Post Malone] has a song for every Spotify playlist imaginable."[10]

***—Al Horner, reviewer for British newspaper the* Guardian**

THE AMERICAN MUSIC AWARDS

The American Music Awards is a fan-voted awards show that airs in more than 160 countries. The nominees are decided by album and song sales, radio plays, streams, and artist tours, which are tracked by *Billboard*. In 2018, actress Tracee Ellis Ross hosted the awards show. Performances included songs by Post Malone, Missy Elliot, Carrie Underwood, Taylor Swift, and Cardi B. Post also received six nominations and two awards.

Mark Wahlberg is an actor and producer who got his start in Hollywood as rapper Marky Mark of Marky Mark and the Funky Bunch.

In addition to performances by Post, there were performances by artists Travis Scott; Tyler, the Creator; Lil Skies; and Ski Mask the Slump God, as well as others. There were also games, food, and other activities.

> **"'Rockstar' and its follow-up single 'Psycho' have an ease to them, an unlikely grace. Each pairs the rapper with a spacious, unhurried beat."[12]**
> **– *Evan Rytlewski,* Pitchfork *reviewer***

After the festival, *Washington Post* writer Jeff Weiss published a negative review that stirred some controversy. In the review, Weiss stated that "Post Malone is a Halloween rental, a removable platinum grill, a Cubic Zirconium proposal on the jumbo screen of a last-place team."[11] Post Malone's father and stepmother both tweeted negative comments about Weiss, and many fans followed suit. However, Post's parents later toned down some of their comments. Post did not comment on the controversy but instead retweeted a positive review of his festival.

Post had his sights set on other things than Twitter feuds. In 2018, he was cast in Mark Wahlberg's movie *Wonderland*, which was produced for Netflix. The movie

ILE 22
MILE
ILE 2

While several of Post's songs mention love interests, he keeps his relationship status very private.

is a film adaptation of writer Ace Atkins's detective novel *Robert B. Parker's Wonderland*. The novel, one of 48 in a series, revolves around conspiracy and murder. It was Post's first acting role. The movie finished filming in December 2018 and was scheduled to debut on Netflix in 2019.

THE PERSONAL SIDE

In late 2018, Post Malone ended a three-year relationship with music promoter and rapper Ashlen Diaz. They began dating in 2015 when Ashlen met Post in Dallas, Texas. Diaz helped Post book concerts and appearances in the early years of his career.

Post kept his relationship out of the public eye as much as possible. He also found that it was difficult working on music and maintaining a relationship at the same time. In an interview, Post said, "It's tough having a balance, between dedicating my life to music and dedicating time for Ashlen.

POST
Better Now

It's tough because you want to get into the studio, you want to do as good music as you can, sometimes you're real busy."[13] Over the years, his relationship with Diaz was observed to be on-again, off-again. They had broken up and gotten back together.

After the breakup with Diaz, Post's dating life became a topic of tabloid and internet gossip rumors. However, as of June 2019, Post had not announced that he was dating anyone else.

As 2019 dawned, it looked like Post Malone's career would continue to accelerate, with plans for a 2019 European tour as well as an adults-only hip-hop

SONGS ABOUT DIAZ

Diaz and Post were together for three years, but they rarely appeared in public together. However, many people speculate that some of Post's songs are about their relationship and eventual split. In "Rich & Sad," Post raps, "I just keep on wishin' that the money made you stay / You ain't never cared about that bulls*** anyway." The song "Stay" includes the lyrics "Every time we make-up, the truth is fadin'."[14] However, Post has not explicitly stated that these songs are about Diaz.

"Give everything a chance, give it a listen, don't judge it off the bat. Let it rock the whole way through."[15]

– Post Malone

In 2018, Post played at the Wireless Festival in London, United Kingdom. He planned to tour Europe in 2019.

cruise with Malone performing. However, Malone has always had more than his share of controversies, and they would continue to be at the forefront of his career.

Stay Away
Always
Tired

Chapter EIGHT

CONTROVERSIES

On February 10, 2019, Post performed with the Red Hot Chili Peppers at the Grammy Awards. He also received four award nominations, though he did not win any Grammys in 2019. Malone was originally supposed to perform with his rap collaborator 21 Savage on the song "Rockstar," but 21 Savage was arrested and detained by US Customs and Immigration in Atlanta, Georgia. Allegedly, 21 Savage, a citizen of the United Kingdom, had overstayed his visa and had never returned to the United Kingdom.

Post Malone performed the song alone, but after his performance he released a photo of himself wearing a 21 Savage T-shirt. He also advertised a petition on Instagram supporting 21 Savage and asking for his release. Some people considered Post's support of 21 Savage controversial, since 21 Savage had allegedly broken immigration laws. Others stood behind Post's support of his fellow rapper and collaborator.

Post has dealt with many controversies during his short time in the spotlight.

Post Malone and the Red Hot Chili Peppers performed a medley of Post's songs and the Red Hot Chili Peppers' songs at the Grammys.

CULTURE VULTURE

Post was no stranger to controversy. Since he first came onto the music scene as a hip-hop artist, people have accused Post of being a "culture vulture" and

appropriating elements of African American and hip-hop culture in order to become successful. Hau Latukefu is the host of the weekly *Hip Hop Show* on Triple J, an Australian radio channel featuring alternative music. Latukefu has said that many people are upset about what Post is doing,

"BLOODY SUNDAY"

In March 2019, white rapper Yelawolf released a YouTube video of him rapping freestyle. The video was called "Bloody Sunday." In it, Yelawolf took shots at just about every other white rapper, including Post Malone, rapping, "Postie, why can't we be friends? / Our clothes already match / Poseur, biter, appropriation thief." Post weighed in on Yelawolf's comments on Twitter: "Also Yelawolf is a nerd, and this tweet is the only support I will offer his album :)." After taking a screenshot of an old Instagram post where Yelawolf had liked one of Post's photos, Post added: "also lmk when your band . . . wants to play some actual good music."[3]

"People are gonna hate you for what they're not gonna understand you for. . . . Especially with the power of music, we can push past the world's flaws and make it a more beautiful place."[4]

–Post Malone

from his hairstyles to his accent to the music that he creates. Latukefu said that people "feel that [Post] has a certain privilege where he can dip into the culture, make a lot of money, and not deal with any kind of real issues that a lot of his black peers are facing."[1]

Some of Post's actions have fed into these accusations over the years. In 2015, he stated, "I'm not a rapper—I'm an artist," as if rappers were not artists.[2] That same year, radio show host Charlamagne tha God asked Post what he was doing for Black Lives Matter, the activist group fighting racial inequality for black people in the United States. Post replied, "I guess what I can do to help Black Lives Matter is keep making music."[5] This statement came under fire from both Charlamagne and also other rappers and fans. Later, Post reflected on his answer. He said, "I wish I'd said [to Charlamagne tha God], 'What are you doing for Black Lives Matter?' . . . Like, maybe my music's not the best, but I know I'm not a bad person, so you're just being a hater."[6]

People also criticized Post for his comments in his 2017 interview with *NewOnce* about hip-hop lacking depth, which seemed to insult the genre of music that had made

Charlamagne tha God hosts the hip-hop radio show *The Breakfast Club*.

him popular and wealthy. He made similar comments during a 2018 *GQ* interview. The interviewer asked him if he ever felt anxious about working in a genre of music that is primarily identified with black artists and black culture. Post replied, "I definitely feel like there's a struggle being a white rapper. But I don't want to be a rapper. I just want to be a person that makes music. I make music that I like and I think that kicks a**, that I think the people who [like] me as a person and as an artist will like."[7]

"The reason why [Post Malone's] sound hits people over the head so hard is that there are country melodies and tones over a hip-hop song."[8]

– *Dre London*

CHARLAMAGNE THA GOD

Charlamagne tha God, born Lenard Larry McKelvey, hosts *The Breakfast Club* on iHeartRadio, as well as the podcast *Brilliant Idiots*. He has written two books, including a memoir and self-help book called *Black Privilege: Opportunity Comes to Those Who Create It*. On his show, Charlamagne tha God discusses hip-hop culture and has interviewed celebrities including Post Malone, Hillary Clinton, and Ava DuVernay.

Many critics say that Post is an example of white fragility. This occurs when white people feel uncomfortable and defensive when they are confronted with the reality of racial inequality and injustice and their place in those systems. In an article for the magazine *Complex*, Shawn Setaro wrote:

> *Post Malone wants the fans . . . and the expensive shoes that come from being a successful rapper. But he also wants to . . . discard the music, the people who make it, and the people who love it as soon as there's a different audience to chase. He feels like he faces difficulties for being white, despite the fact that [his whiteness] gave him access to a mass audience few of his peers can touch.*[9]

GUNS AND POLITICS

Post has also created controversy because of his progun stance toward gun control. He enjoys visiting shooting ranges, and he has stated, "The feeling [of shooting a gun] is pure . . . inebriation. It's like hitting a punching bag to let off steam."[10] Post owns many guns. In a 2017 interview with *Rolling Stone*, he showed the writer his extensive collection of guns. He said, "They're fun, they're practical, and bad s*** happens. If you hurt me, I'm gonna hurt you back."[11]

In December 2016, during an interview with Charlamagne tha God on *The Breakfast Club* radio program, Post Malone talked about politics, voting, and Donald Trump, who was president-elect at the time. Post stated that he didn't vote in the 2016 election because "our votes are suggestions to the Electoral College."[12] He also stated that while he didn't feel either candidate (Donald Trump or Hillary Clinton) was fit for the office of president, he would have played for Trump's inauguration if he were asked. Malone first joked, "How much money is it?" He then added, "If he was to say, 'Yo, I really like your music. Can you come and do a show?' Why would I

POST MALONE, CONSPIRACY THEORIST

Post Malone believes in several conspiracy theories about politics and the government. He told *Rolling Stone*, "There's crazy s*** that goes on that we can't explain. Chemtrails and s***."[13] According to conspiracy theorists, contrails—the condensed water that appears as streaks of white substances in the sky behind a plane or rocket—are actually "chemtrails." These chemtrails supposedly release chemicals into the atmosphere in order to control people. The theory of chemtrails has been disproven by many scientists and aviation experts. Other conspiracy theories that Post believes include that the US government plotted the assassination of President John F. Kennedy, that a type of secret gun can cause heart attacks, and that the world could end at any moment.

get backlash because of someone booking me? . . . If I do his show, does that mean I'm a supporter of him?"[14] Later in the interview, Post claimed that he was only joking. However, according to the political journalism website 71Republic, Post received negative feedback from many of his fans for his comments. In November 2017, he stated in an interview with *Rolling Stone* that "we have a sh**** thing going on in the White House—I don't like Trump. But I don't think it's just him."[15]

In just a few years, Post went from being a young man from Texas trying to make it in the music business to an internationally known hip-hop artist. And even though he is known for the many controversies that surround him, he has already made a lasting impact on the music world.

SUCCEEDING DESPITE CONTROVERSY

Post Malone has many critics who accuse him of appropriating African American culture. Other critics say he's getting more attention than his talent deserves. But despite these criticisms, Post continues to succeed. According to Rob Stevenson, an executive at Republic Records, "Things that should've killed his career have only made him bigger."[16]

Chapter NINE

A WORLD MUSICIAN

One thing that's clear about Post's future is that he will continue to reject all genre labels that people try to put on him or his music. In a 2017 interview, Post said that "genre is stupid."[1] He sees no problem moving from hip-hop singles with 21 Savage to pop songs with Justin Bieber, as well as recording songs that are more country and western or folk.

While some reviewers have criticized him for this mix of genres, others feel that he has taken hip-hop and repurposed it with less of a dark edge. As Lindsay Zoladz of the sports and pop culture website the Ringer commented, "He's packaging something that's a little bit more controversial and confrontational in a friendlier pop package."[2] Post has weighed in on the discussion too, saying, "I wanna take this genre and stretch it so far that people who may not listen to it, listen to it."[3] There is no

Post attended the premiere of *Into the Spider-Verse* with rapper and collaborator Swae Lee, *left*.

"My last hip-hop album was f**** hip-hop. My next hip-hop album is f****** hip-hop. I love hip-hop. I make hip-hop."[5]**

– Post Malone

DEMOGRAPHICS

Post began moving into the rap music genre when he was in high school, but he didn't share his music with his parents or invite them to his rap performances, even though they'd attended his rock performances before. It wasn't until his dad came across Post's rap mixtape that he heard Malone's new genre. "I don't want to say I was mad, but I was mad. All the things you think of with a kid like Post, with his demographic, those things go through a dad's head with the challenges he's going to face," his dad, Rich, told the *Dallas Observer*.[6] He knew that someone like Post, in the hip-hop music business, would be facing criticism as a white man in a largely black music genre.

question, judging by Post's list of awards and albums selling in record numbers, that his genre-defying music is popular, regardless of what some critics say.

STREAMING AND POPULARITY

Music streaming has been an asset to Post's career. He broke the record on Spotify for most streams of an album in a week when *Beerbongs & Bentleys* was streamed 431 million times worldwide in its first week of release. At the end of 2017, Post was called "the most streamed artist in the world" when his songs held the top position at both Spotify and Apple Music.[4] Post also made the Spotify list of artists who were most streamed in 2018.

Streaming has changed the way musical artists reach the top of music charts and stay there. Post's music has the ability to reach the charts based on how people listen to it on streaming services. However, critics are quick to point out that the number of times a song or album is streamed doesn't necessarily mean that it's popular with fans. Some music is downloaded because it is controversial or even laughingly bad, and once it goes viral, people may only download it based on curiosity. However, it also means that musicians can attract listeners from

CHILLHOP

Some people say that Post's music puts them in a trance. This is perhaps what has made his music so popular on streaming programs like Spotify. Liz Pelly, writing on *The Baffler* website, believes that streaming playlists "have spawned a new type of music listener, one who thinks less about the artist or album they are seeking out, and instead connects with emotions, moods and activities, where they just pick a playlist and let it roll." These services, according to Lindsay Zoladz, have turned "listening into more of a passive, background activity."[7]

One emerging genre that has come out of music streaming is called chillhop. Chillhop features lo-fi hip-hop beats and elements of smooth jazz, as well as other downtempo pieces of electronica and R&B. Chillhop music is mostly intended to fade into the background. Some of Post Malone's music, such as "Rockstar," include elements of chillhop. The genre is popular on streaming services such as YouTube and Spotify.

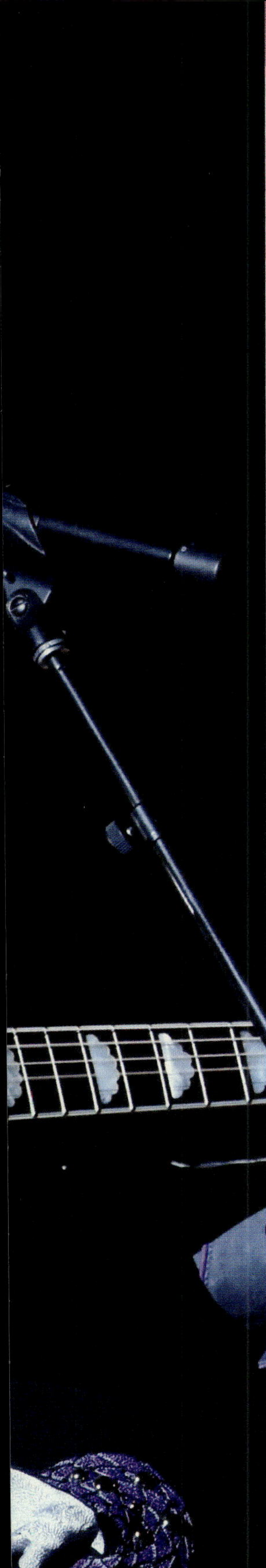

All of Post's released music, including his acoustic songs, is available on streaming services such as Spotify and Apple Music.

a wider range of people, since it can be easier to access music using a streaming service than by purchasing individual songs or albums.

The structure of Malone's songs also helps them top the streaming charts. If someone streams a song on a streaming service for only 30 seconds, it still counts as one stream. Because Malone's songs are written with a catchy "hook" at the beginning, it makes it more likely that the listener will stay with the song for that crucial 30 seconds.

However, some critics accused "Rockstar" of being unfairly boosted up in those charts by YouTube. Republic Records, Post's label, put a portion of the song on YouTube. The video consisted of only the chorus of "Rockstar" looping over and over again for the full length of the actual song. Views of this video were counted as part of the streaming totals for "Rockstar," which in turn count toward placement on the charts. People who view YouTube on autoplay, where an algorithm plays additional songs based on what the listener has previously listened to, will also hear the song clip without realizing it, which still counts toward the number of overall streams.

VOODOO MUSIC AND ARTS EXPERIENCE

Voodoo Music and Arts Experience is a music festival in October in New Orleans, Louisiana. In June 2019 it was announced that Post Malone would headline the second night of the festival that year. The other headliners were Guns N' Roses and Beck. Post had previously played the festival in 2017, but he was headlining the festival for the first time in 2019. The *New Orleans Advocate* stated that the three headliners were meant to draw different crowds and demographics of people to the festival. Journalist Keith Spera noted, "Guns N' Roses is for parents who like loud guitars. Post Malone is for teens and 20-somethings who don't. Beck falls somewhere in the middle."[8]

WHAT'S NEXT FOR POST MALONE?

With all his success, it is natural that many people are wondering what is next for Malone. He has managed to defeat the accusations of being a one-hit wonder, but that means he will need to continue writing and performing hit songs and albums. In June 2018, Post promised he was already working on his next album, saying in a Twitter post: "i am writing for

Post Malone toured around the world in 2019 and played festivals such as Lollapalooza in Brazil.

the next album. thank u to everyone who is listening. . . . i love u."[9]

However, a new album may take a while for Post to record. Rumors about Post starting his own label, or appearing in more movies, have circulated on the internet. Post's manager, Dre London, fed into those rumors. He told *Billboard* that Post has "seen the music business inside out and now he wants to start his label." London also said, to support rumors about a film career, that "Post has . . . a great movie idea, and I've been begging him to play a role in it because he's good at acting. . . . [Post] wants to do . . .

Post Malone's set at the 2019 Bonnaroo Music and Arts Festival in Tennessee included many pyrotechnic effects.

stuff that we own, where a part of that comes from our vision, our creation."[10]

Even though Post is an award-winning artist, he still finds time to connect with his fans using social media.

In early March 2019, a 40-year-old man named Mike Alancourt from a Florida dance studio posted a video of himself on Instagram doing a dance routine to Post's song "Wow." Post re-uploaded the video on his own

In his spare time, Post sometimes attends Dallas Cowboys football games.

Instagram the next day with the caption "This is so F****** AWESOME!!"[11] Post later flew Alancourt to Phoenix, Arizona, to do some background dancing at Post's concert. Film segments of Alancourt were also added to the music video for "Wow."

It's clear that Post has many plans for the future. He will continue to make music across genres and also expand his presence into movies, television, record producing, and much more. He's just getting started. As he says, "So long as I keep making good music, everything's going to be OK."[12]

POST MALONE DEFENDS LIL NAS X

In 2019, rapper Lil Nas X's song "Old Town Road" became famous when country artist Billy Ray Cyrus was featured on the remix. The song reached the top of the country music charts before it was removed from the list. Some claimed this was because the song wasn't country enough for the country charts. Other people had a problem with Lil Nas X creating a country song because he was a rapper. When Lil Nas X rapped about wearing Wrangler jeans, some country music fans decided to boycott the brand. Celebrity gossip website TMZ asked Post Malone if he had any opinions about the "Old Town Road" controversy. Referring to Lil Nas X, Post repeated what he often says about his own tendency to blend genres: "I think people should be able to, you know . . . make whatever [music] they want to. . . . I mean, music's just f****** music."[13]

TIMELINE

1995

Austin Richard Post is born on July 4 in Syracuse, New York.

2008

Post wins his eighth grade talent show singing a metalcore cover version of the Rihanna song "Umbrella."

2010

Post auditions for the rock band Crown the Empire but is rejected.

2013

Post, who has now created the stage name Post Malone, graduates from high school in Grapevine, Texas.

2014

Post and several other musicians and producers form the group BLKCVRD in Los Angeles, California.

Post and other members of BLKCVRD move into a mansion in Encino, California, nicknamed the White House.

2015

Post writes the song "White Iverson."

Post signs with Republic Records.

In August, Post performs at Kylie Jenner's eighteenth birthday party and meets Kanye West.

2016

Post tours with Justin Bieber on his Purpose World Tour.

On April 21, Post previews his new single, "Go Flex," on the Beats 1 show.

Post's first mixtape, *August 26*, is released on May 12.

In June, Post makes his television debut on *Jimmy Kimmel Live!*

On August 26, Post's first album, *Stoney*, is released.

2017

In September, Post releases the song "Rockstar" with 21 Savage.

2018

Post breaks records for the most songs in the top 20 of the Hot 100 at the same time.

In April, Post's second album, *Beerbongs & Bentleys*, debuts and sets a streaming record in its first week.

2019

Post performs at the Grammy awards after receiving four nominations.

Post was set to go on a world tour for *Beerbongs & Bentleys*.

ESSENTIAL FACTS

FULL NAME

Austin Richard Post

DATE OF BIRTH

July 4, 1995

PLACE OF BIRTH

Syracuse, New York

PARENTS

Rich Post and stepmother Jodie Post

EDUCATION

Graduated from Grapevine High School in Grapevine, Texas, in 2013.

CAREER HIGHLIGHTS

Post Malone rose to fame when his song "White Iverson" went viral in 2015. In 2018, he broke the record for having the most songs in the top 20 of the *Billboard* Hot 100 at the same time. In 2019, Post was nominated for four Grammy Awards.

ALBUMS

August 26 (2016), *Stoney* (2016), *Beerbongs & Bentleys* (2018)

CONTRIBUTION TO HIP-HOP

Post blends many different musical genres into his songs, giving hip-hop his own unique flavor and attracting new listeners.

CONFLICTS

Post's identification as a white rapper and the accusations by the hip-hop and music industries that he is a "culture vulture" have been controversial, as well as his interview quote that if listeners are looking for music with lyrics and thoughts about life, they should not be listening to hip-hop.

QUOTE

"I think it's time for a change. We need to turn up on 'em. Real quick."

—Post Malone, speaking about including acoustic and folk sounds in his music, 2017

GLOSSARY

ANCESTRY

A person's family or ethnic background.

BACKLASH

A strong and adverse reaction to a social or political event by a large number of people.

BLURRING

Making something less distinct or clear.

COLLABORATION

Multiple artists working together on a single track or album.

DEBUT

To make a first appearance.

DISC JOCKEY (DJ)

A person who introduces and plays recorded music, such as on the radio or at an event.

GENRE

A specific type of music, film, or writing.

JAM

To improvise music with other musicians in an informal setting.

LO-FI

Short for "low fidelity," a style of music in which the audio recording is purposefully of low quality, which allows for audible scratches and background noise.

MIXTAPE

A compilation of unreleased tracks, freestyle rap music, and DJ mixes of songs.

STREAMING

A way to transmit or receive data, often music, over a computer network, which allows playback to start before all the data is transmitted.

SYNTHESIZER

An electronic musical instrument, usually with a keyboard, that can make a wide variety of sounds by combining signals of different frequencies.

ADDITIONAL RESOURCES

SELECTED BIBLIOGRAPHY

Hyman, Dan. "Explaining Post Malone: Why Is the Rapper So Popular?" *Chicago Tribune*, 31 May 2018, chicagotribune.com. Accessed 22 Apr. 2019.

Lui, Herbert. "Post Malone on Teaching Himself Guitar, Making Music with No Money, and Working with Kanye West." *HuffPost*, 2 Dec. 2016, huffingtonpost.com. Accessed 22 Apr. 2019.

Stephen, Bijan. "Don't Call Post Malone a Rapper." *GQ*, 25 Jan. 2018, gq.com. Accessed 22 Apr. 2019.

FURTHER READINGS

Cummings, Judy Dodge. *Hip-Hop Culture*. Abdo, 2018.

Lusted, Marcia Amidon. *Hip-Hop Music*. Abdo, 2018.

ONLINE RESOURCES

Booklinks
NONFICTION NETWORK
FREE! ONLINE NONFICTION RESOURCES

To learn more about Post Malone, please visit **abdobooklinks.com** or scan this QR code. These links are routinely monitored and updated to provide the most current information available.

MORE INFORMATION

For more information on this subject, please contact or visit the following organizations:

HIP HOP CAUCUS
1638 R St. NW, #120
Washington, DC 20009
hiphopcaucus.org

Hip Hop Caucus uses hip-hop culture and cultural expression to empower communities that are most impacted by injustice. Its political campaigns and projects involve members from all over the world, including students.

HIP HOP FOR CHANGE
517 Fifty-Fifth St.
Oakland, CA 94609
hiphopforchange.org

Hip Hop for Change is a nonprofit foundation that uses hip-hop culture to educate people about social injustice and find solutions.

UNIVERSAL HIP HOP MUSEUM
PO Box 6001
Bronx, NY 10451
uhhm.org

The Universal Hip Hop Museum is the official museum for hip-hop music. Opening in 2022, it will create educational experiences around the hip-hop culture of the past, present, and future.

SOURCE NOTES

CHAPTER 1. NEW AND OLD

1. Daniel Kreps and Sarah Grant. "Watch Aerosmith, Post Malone, 21 Savage Close Out MTV VMAs with 'Toys in the Attic.'" *Rolling Stone*, 21 Aug. 2018, rollingstone.com. Accessed 17 July 2019.
2. Kreps and Grant, "Watch Aerosmith, Post Malone, 21 Savage."
3. Matthew Lurie. "KRS-One Spreads Refreshing Message." *Chicago Tribune*, 18 Oct. 2004, chicagotribune.com. Accessed 17 July 2019.
4. Carl Lamarre. "Post Malone on the Early Success of 'Rockstar.'" *Billboard*, 28 Sept. 2017, billboard.com. Accessed 17 July 2019.
5. Bijan Stephen. "Don't Call Post Malone a Rapper." *GQ*, 25 Jan. 2018, gq.com. Accessed 17 July 2019.
6. Stephen, "Don't Call Post Malone a Rapper."
7. Gaby Wilson. "Why Is Post Malone So D*** Catchy?" *Vice*, 11 Nov. 2018, vice.com. Accessed 17 July 2019.
8. Lamarre, "Post Malone on the Early Success of 'Rockstar.'"

CHAPTER 2. BECOMING POST

1. Geoff Herbert. "Rapper Post Malone's Father Talks Syracuse Roots, Musical Influences—and Haters." *Syracuse.com*, 20 Oct. 2017, syracuse.com. Accessed 17 July 2019.
2. Herbert, "Rapper Post Malone's Father Talks Syracuse Roots."
3. Justin Ivey. "Post Malone Claims *Guitar Hero* Helped Start His Music Career." *XXL*, 9 Feb. 2016, xxlmag.com. Accessed 17 July 2019.
4. Ivey, "Post Malone Claims *Guitar Hero* Helped Start His Music Career."
5. Herbert, "Rapper Post Malone's Father Talks Syracuse Roots."
6. Georgia Straub. "I Taught Post Malone." *Timber Creek Talon*, 29 Aug. 2018, timbercreektalon.com. Accessed 17 July 2019.
7. Herbert Lui. "Post Malone on Teaching Himself Guitar, Making Music with No Money, and Working with Kanye West." *HuffPost*, 21 June 2017, huffpost.com. Accessed 17 July 2019.
8. Herbert, "Rapper Post Malone's Father Talks Syracuse Roots."
9. Erin Vanderhoof. "Post Malone . . . Goes Far-Out on *Beerbongs & Bentleys*." *Vanity Fair*, 27 Apr. 2018, vanityfair.com. Accessed 17 July 2019.
10. Zara Golden. "How Post Malone Became the Most Random Success in Rap." *Fader*, 14 May 2015, thefader.com. Accessed 17 July 2019.
11. Jordan Zirm. "Everything You Need to Know about Post Malone." *Complex*, 6 Sept. 2018, complex.com. Accessed 17 July 2019.

CHAPTER 3. LEAVING FOR LOS ANGELES

1. Herbert Lui. "Post Malone on Teaching Himself Guitar, Making Music with No Money, and Working with Kanye West." *HuffPost*, 21 June 2017, huffpost.com. Accessed 17 July 2019.
2. @actually_posty [Post Malone secondary account]. "I didn't go to Syracuse. . . ." *Twitter*, 17 Dec. 2017, 2:23 p.m. twitter.com. Accessed 24 July 2019.
3. Lui, "Post Malone on Teaching Himself Guitar."
4. "Billie Gvtes." *SoundCloud*, n.d., soundcloud.com. Accessed 17 July 2019.
5. Gail Mitchell. "Producer FKi 1st Talks Diplo, Post Malone and 'The First Time for Everything.'" *Billboard*, 25 Feb. 2016, billboard.com. Accessed 17 July 2019.
6. Lui, "Post Malone on Teaching Himself Guitar."
7. Lui, "Post Malone on Teaching Himself Guitar."
8. Lui, "Post Malone on Teaching Himself Guitar."
9. Lui, "Post Malone on Teaching Himself Guitar."

CHAPTER 4. CLIMBING THE LADDER

1. Colin Stutz. "Post Malone's Manager Dre London on Secrets to Success." *Billboard*, 22 May 2018, billboard.com. Accessed 17 July 2019.
2. Stutz, "Post Malone's Manager Dre London on Secrets to Success."
3. @PostMalone. "If y'all are actually my fans and friends and love me . . ." *Twitter*, 6 Jan. 2019, 7:31 a.m. twitter.com. Accessed 17 July 2019.

4. Adelle Platon. "Rapper Post Malone on Collaborating with Kanye West." *Billboard*, 14 Dec. 2015, billboard.com. Accessed 17 July 2019.
5. Kameron Hay. "How Post Malone Blew Up." *Complex*, 16 May 2018, complex.com. Accessed 17 July 2019.
6. Matthew Ramirez. "Post Malone: *Stoney*." *Pitchfork*, 15 Dec. 2016, pitchfork.com. Accessed 17 July 2019.
7. Carl Lamarre. "Post Malone Still Thinks 'White Iverson' Is His Only 'Good Song.'" *Billboard*, 11 Dec. 2017, billboard.com. Accessed 17 July 2019.
8. Platon, "Rapper Post Malone on Collaborating with Kanye West."
9. "Fade: Kanye West." *Genius*, n.d., genius.com. Accessed 17 July 2019.
10. "Fade: Kanye West."

CHAPTER 5. OUT IN THE WORLD

1. Jeff Gage. "Post Malone Drops New Track and Talks about Life on the Road with Justin Bieber." *Dallas Observer*, 22 Apr. 2016, dallasobserver.com. Accessed 17 July 2019.
2. Jason Lipshutz. "Here's How Many Days Justin Bieber Has Had Off Since His Purpose Tour Began." *Billboard*, 25 July 2017, billboard.com. Accessed 19 July 2019.
3. Gage, "Post Malone Drops New Track."
4. Kaitlyn Frey. "Post Malone Jokes He Got His First Tattoo to Prove He Was 'Way Tougher' Than Justin Bieber." *People*, 2 Oct. 2018, people.com. Accessed 17 July 2019.
5. Joshua Copperman. "Justin Bieber and Post Malone's Beautiful Bromance." *Spin*, 20 Aug. 2018, spin.com. Accessed 17 July 2019.
6. Copperman, "Justin Bieber and Post Malone's Beautiful Bromance."
7. "Justin Bieber Bros Down with Post Malone." *Blast*, 29 June 2018, theblast.com. Accessed 26 Aug. 2019.
8. Gage, "Post Malone Drops New Track."
9. Victoria Hernandez. "Post Malone Ignored XXL Freshmen." *Hip Hop DX*, 16 June 2016, hiphopdx.com. Accessed 17 July 2019.
10. Jonah Weiner. "Post Malone: Confessions of a Hip-Hop Rock Star." *Rolling Stone*, 17 Nov. 2017, rollingstone.com. Accessed 17 July 2019.
11. Jessie Morris. "Post Malone Drops His New Song 'Go Flex.'" *Complex*, 21 Apr. 2016, complex.com. Accessed 17 July 2019.
12. Matthew Ramirez. "Post Malone: *Stoney*." *Pitchfork*, 15 Dec. 2016, pitchfork.com. Accessed 17 July 2019.
13. Sebastian. "Post Malone: *Stoney*." *Sputnikmusic*, 6 Aug. 2017, sputnikmusic.com. Accessed 17 July 2019.
14. Hernandez, "Post Malone Ignored XXL Freshmen."

CHAPTER 6. ALBUMS, INTERVIEWS, AND ACCIDENTS

1. Ben Dandridge-Lemco. "Post Malone: 'If You're Looking to Think about Life. . .'" *Fader*, 20 Nov. 2017, thefader.com. Accessed 19 July 2019.
2. Trace Williams. "Vince Staples Wonders if Future's Verse on '3500' Would Make Post Malone Cry." *Complex*, 24 Nov. 2017, complex.com. Accessed 19 July 2019.
3. @XLNB. "Post Malone's comments are a shallow analysis of hip hop. . ." *Twitter*, 22 Nov. 2017, 11:38 a.m. twitter.com. Accessed 19 July 2019.
4. Shakiel Mahjouri. "Post Malone Blames Anti-Hip Hop Tirade on 'A Lot of Beer in My Face.'" *ET Canada*, 23 Nov. 2017, etcanada.com. Accessed 19 July 2019.
5. Andrew Marantz. "The Dumb Brilliance of Lil B." *New Yorker*, 13 Apr. 2012, newyorker.com. Accessed 19 July 2019.
6. Abel Shifferaw. "Lil B Went Off on Post Malone." *Complex*, 6 Oct. 2017, complex.com. Accessed 19 July 2019.
7. Mahjouri, "Post Malone Blames Anti-Hip Hop Tirade on 'A Lot of Beer.'"
8. Chris Jordan, "Post Malone: Meet the Grammy-Nominated Perth Amboy Engineer Who Helped Record 'Rockstar.'" *Asbury Park Press*, 6 Feb. 2019, app.com. Accessed 19 July 2019.
9. Carl Lamarre. "Post Malone on the Early Success of 'Rockstar.'" *Billboard*, 28 Sept. 2017, billboard.com. Accessed 17 July 2019.

CONTINUED

SOURCE NOTES

10. Meaghan Garvey. "Review: Post Malone's 'Beerbongs & Bentleys' Is a Flexing, Partying Rich-Sad Bummer." *Rolling Stone*, 1 May 2018, rollingstone.com. Accessed 19 July 2019.

11. Andrew Unterberger. "Post Malone's 'Beerbongs and Bentleys' Will Silence Some Naysayers, But Not the Ones He Should Actually Listen To." *Billboard*, 27 Apr. 2018, billboard.com. Accessed 19 July 2019.

12. Lauren Tingle. "Keith Urban and Post Malone Connect over Elvis." *CMT*, 19 Mar. 2019, cmt.com. Accessed 19 July 2019.

13. Colin Stutz. "Post Malone's Manager Dre London on Secrets to Success." *Billboard*, 22 May 2018, billboard.com. Accessed 17 July 2019.

14. Isabel Torrealba. "Here Are All the Terrible Things That Have Happened to Post Malone Lately." *Slate*, 10 Sept. 2018, slate.com. Accessed 19 July 2019.

15. Torrealba, "Here Are All the Terrible Things That Have Happened to Post Malone Lately."

16. Rebecca Schiller. "Watch Post Malone Discuss Emergency Plane Landing." *Billboard*, 4 Oct. 2018, billboard.com. Accessed 19 July 2019.

CHAPTER 7. HIP-HOP AND HOLLYWOOD

1. Jon Blistein. "Post Malone Previews New 'Spiderman' Song 'Sunflower' on 'Fallon.'" *Rolling Stone*, 2 Oct. 2018, rollingstone.com. Accessed 19 July 2019.

2. Blistein, "Post Malone Previews New 'Spiderman' Song."

3. Katie Kilkenny. "Jimmy Fallon Eats Olive Garden for First Time with Connoisseur Post Malone." *Billboard*, 12 Oct. 2018, billboard.com. Accessed 19 July 2019.

4. Kilkenny, "Jimmy Fallon Eats Olive Garden."

5. Lena Grossman. "Post Malone Makes Drastic Change to His Appearance." *E News Online*, 8 Oct. 2018, eonline.com. Accessed 19 July 2019.

6. Kilkenny, "Jimmy Fallon Eats Olive Garden."

7. Grossman, "Post Malone Makes Drastic Change."

8. "Watch: Jimmy Fallon and Post Malone Sing Irish Tunes in NYC Pub." *IrishCentral*, 4 Oct. 2018, irishcentral.com. Accessed 19 July 2019.

9. QCWriter. "Post Malone Receives Major Criticism over AMAs Performance." *Hot 96.9 Boston*, 9 Oct. 2018, hot969boston.com. Accessed 19 July 2019.

10. Al Horner. "Post Malone Review." *Guardian*, 18 Feb. 2019, theguardian.com. Accessed 19 July 2019.

11. Susanna Heller. "Post Malone and His Family Apparently Encouraged Fans to Harass a Journalist after a Negative Review of Posty Fest." *Insider*, 5 Nov. 2018, insider.com. Accessed 19 July 2019.

12. Evan Rytlewski. "Post Malone: *Beerbongs & Bentleys*." *Pitchfork*, 3 May 2018, pitchfork.com. Accessed 19 July 2019.

13. Dan Clarendon. "Post Malone and Girlfriend Ashlen Diaz Break Up after Three Years Together." *US Weekly*, 2 Nov. 2018, usmagazine.com. Accessed 19 July 2019.

14. Effie Orfanides. "Ashlen Diaz, Post Malone's Girlfriend." *Heavy*, 21 Aug. 2018, heavy.com. Accessed 19 July 2019.

15. Herbert Lui. "Post Malone on Teaching Himself Guitar, Making Music with No Money, and Working with Kanye West." *HuffPost*, 21 June 2017, huffpost.com. Accessed 17 July 2019.

CHAPTER 8. CONTROVERSIES

1. Paul Donoughue. "Post Malone: The Complicated Appeal of the US Singer Breaking Chart Records around the World." *ABC News Online*, 11 May 2018, abc.net.au. Accessed 22 July 2019.

2. Shawn Setaro. "Here's Why Post Malone Is a Problem." *Complex*, 27 Nov. 2017, complex.com. Accessed 21 July 2019.

3. Michael Saponara. "Post Malone Fires Back at Yelawolf Following 'Bloody Sunday' Diss." *Billboard*, 13 Mar. 2019, billboard.com. Accessed 21 July 2019.

4. Jonah Weiner. "Post Malone: Confessions of a Hip-Hop Rock Star." *Rolling Stone*, 17 Nov. 2017, rollingstone.com. Accessed 21 July 2019.

5. Weiner, "Post Malone."

6. Weiner, "Post Malone."

7. Bijan Stephen. "Don't Call Post Malone a Rapper." *GQ*, 25 Jan. 2018, gq.com. Accessed 21 July 2019.

8. Jayson Greene. "Learning to Love Post Malone." *Pitchfork*, 26 July 2018, pitchfork.com. Accessed 21 July 2019.

9. Setaro, "Here's Why Post Malone Is a Problem."

10. Weiner, "Post Malone."

11. Weiner, "Post Malone."

12. Jenna Romaine. "Post Malone Talks JFK Assassination and Trump Inauguration on 'The Breakfast Club.'" *Billboard*, 21 Dec. 2016, billboard.com. Accessed 21 July 2019.

13. Weiner, "Post Malone."

14. Romaine, "Post Malone Talks JFK Assassination."

15. Weiner, "Post Malone."

16. Mikael Wood. "Why Post Malone Has Been Called 'The Donald Trump of Hip-Hop.'" *Los Angeles Times*, 16 Dec. 2016, latimes.com. Accessed 21 July 2019.

CHAPTER 9. A WORLD MUSICIAN

1. Jonah Weiner. "Post Malone: Confessions of a Hip-Hop Rock Star." *Rolling Stone*, 17 Nov. 2017, rollingstone.com. Accessed 21 July 2019.

2. Dan Hyman. "Explaining Post Malone: Why Is the Rapper So Popular?" *Chicago Tribune*, 31 May 2018, chicagotribune.com. Accessed 21 July 2019.

3. Lindsay Zoladz. "The Empty Calories of Post Malone's Beer Bro Rap." *Ringer*, 16 May 2018, theringer.com. Accessed 21 July 2019.

4. "Post Malone Is Currently the 'Most Streamed Artist in the World.'" *Rap-Up*, 11 Oct. 2017, rap-up.com. Accessed 21 July 2019.

5. Trace William Cowen. "Post Malone Clears Up His Controversial Hip-Hop Comments." *Complex*, 23 Nov. 2017, complex.com. Accessed 21 July 2019.

6. Jeff Gage. "Post Malone Drops New Track and Talks about Life on the Road with Justin Bieber." *Dallas Observer*, 22 Apr. 2016, dallasobserver.com. Accessed 21 July 2019.

7. Liz Pelly. "The Problem with Muzak." *Baffler*, December 2017, thebaffler.com. Accessed 21 July 2019.

8. Keith Spera. "Do You Prefer Guns N' Roses or Post Malone? At Voodoo, It's Probably about Your Age." *New Orleans Advocate*, 5 June 2019, nola.com. Accessed 21 July 2019.

9. Matthew Parizot. "Post Malone Is Already Working on His Next Album." *Hot New Hip Hop*, 5 June 2018, hotnewhiphop.com. Accessed 21 July 2019.

10. Colin Stutz. "Post Malone's Manager Dre London on Secrets to Success." *Billboard*, 22 May 2018, billboard.com. Accessed 21 July 2019.

11. "Post Malone Flew Viral 'Wow' Dancer out for Concert and New Music Video." *TMZ*, 20 Mar. 2019, tmz.com. Accessed 21 July 2019.

12. Gage, "Post Malone Drops New Track."

13. "Post Malone Says Country Fans Should Get Off Lil Nas X's A** over Wranglers." *TMZ*, 26 May 2019, tmz.com. Accessed 21 July 2019.

INDEX

ABOUT THE AUTHOR

Marcia Amidon Lusted has written 180 books and more than 600 magazine articles for young readers. She is also an editor and a musician, and she has previously written books about hip-hop as well as the music industry.